My Consecration to Mary

Introduction and Preparation for
the Total Consecration to the Blessed Virgin Mary,
according to Louis Marie Grignion de Montfort.

For Children

Rege, O Maria

Rev. Fr. Bernardo M. Ibarra, IVE

Illustrations by Sr. María Jednosti, SSVM

IVE Press-2021

RELIGIOUS FAMILY OF THE INCARNATE WORD

Nihil Obstat

    R.F. Andrés Bonello, IVE, Provincial Superior

    Provincia "Nuestra Señora de Loreto"

    Institute of the Incarnate Word

Cover Design

    © IVE Press - 2021

Cover Art

    © IVE Press - 2021

    Sr. María Jednosti, SSVM

Interior Art

    © IVE Press – 2021

    Sr. María Jednosti, SSVM

Text

    © Institute of the Incarnate Word

    All rights reserved.

    Fr. Bernardo María del Corazón de Jesús Ibarra, IVE

Manufactured in the United States of America.

IVE Press

    5706 Sargent Rd.

    Chilum, MD 20782

    E-mail: ivepress@ive.org

    http://www.ivepress.org

ISBN-13: 978-1-947568-24-2

Library of Congress Control Number: 2021906944

PROLOGUE

Each person must "manage in every way possible to instill in the hearts of young people a filial devotion to Mary Most Holy"[1], said our beloved St. John Bosco. Since "just as in the natural order, every child must have a father and a mother, in the same way, in the order of grace, a true child of the Church must have God for his Father and Mary for his Mother."[2]

Inspired by filial love for the Blessed Virgin Mary and with the creativity that makes the missionary "weak to win the weak"[3], the author of this valuable book, *My Consecration to Mary*, offers an instrument as equally useful for parents, catechists, and pastors, as for young children, to consecrate themselves to Mary according to the spirit of St. Louis Marie Grignion de Montfort.

The beautifully illustrated pages and simple, catechetical language of this book, present all the tenderness and richness of the true devotion to Mary Most Holy. As a child receives all his nutrition from the mother, who gives to him according to his needs, in the same way the children reading this book will be nourished by Mary, who is "the Children's bread,"[4] as taught by St. Louis Marie.

---

1   *St. John Bosco, Regolamento dell'Oratorio di San Francesco di Sales per gli esterni* (1877), ch. 1, art. 1 and 7
2   St. Louis Marie Grignion de Montfort, The Secret of Mary, 11.
3   1 Corinthians 9:22
4   St. Louis Marie Grignion de Montfort, The Secret of Mary, 20.

Faithful to the Monfortian method, and yet written in a brief manner with important catechetical notes and filial piety to the Mother of God, *My Consecration to Mary* reminds us that the consecration to the Blessed Virgin Mary is the easiest and fastest way to reach Jesus and offers children an exciting way to participate in this centuries-old practice. In just a few days they will come to know the Blessed Mother like never before and take her hand to reach Christ.

Additionally, Fr. Ibarra has filled his book with concrete examples of virtue taken from the lives of saints in order to awaken in the child holy ideals as they grow in childlike piety. These acts of piety, such as bringing flowers to Our Lady, lighting a candle near her as a gift, or reciting short prayers contribute to instill in the young child a holy and true devotion to the Mother of God.

Finally, we consider *My Consecration to Mary* to be a work of great devotional and religious value for young children. If the consecration to Our Lady in maternal slavery of love is embraced wholeheartedly since childhood, it not only has an individual sanctifying efficacy, but is the "mustard seed"[5] the Gospel speaks of for the establishment of the Kingdom of Christ.

St. John Paul II said: "Mary, the Mother of Jesus, in the course of history, has not failed to show her motherly care for the little ones."[6] So we hope the tenderness and simplicity of Marian spirituality children find in reading these pages will allow them to move forward confidently from Mary's hand toward the heavenly homeland, to which we all aspire. This is the main path on which we must educate our children and young people, because to consecrate themselves to Mary is to consecrate themselves to Jesus Christ, to whom She is inseparably united.

Fr. Gustavo Nieto, IVE

---

5   Mt 13:31; Mk 4:3

6   Pope St. John Paul II, Letter to Children in the Year of the Family (December 13, 1994)

INTRODUCTION
FOR PARENTS, TUTORS, AND CATECHISTS

This book is for children and has one goal: to increase devotion to the Blessed Virgin Mary in the souls of children, so that, already in their early childhood, they will be aware of the very important role she plays in their lives as Mother and Queen. Mother, because she conceives in faith, nourishes in hope, and educates in charity. Queen, because she conquered us in union with her most loving Son. We owe everything to her: *totus tuus.*

According to St. Louis Marie Grignion de Montfort, devotion to Mary is tender, "that is to say, full of confidence in her, like a child's confidence in his beloved mother." Therefore, devotion to Our Lady can be lived so particularly by children, who because they are young, are more in need of a mother. This devotion, then, is very appropriate for children. In addition, this devotion makes Mary "an ordinary resource," says the saint, which makes her even more suitable for children, who constantly turn to their elders for help.

Moreover, this devotion penetrates the soul of the child and fills him with supernatural vision. It elevates his aspirations and sets him on a sure path to holiness. St. Thérèse of the Child Jesus, St. John Bosco, St. Aloysius Gonzaga, Padre Pio and St. Louis Marie Grignion de Montfort himself, were great lovers of Our Lady from childhood. Similarly, the little shepherds of Fatima are a perfect example of this tender devotion to Mary, and there are many others like them.

St. Louis Marie was certainly thinking of children when he wrote his famous book Treatise on True Devotion, and he had no doubt that they could become great lovers of Mary. In fact, the book is addressed "in a special way to the humble and simple." Moreover, this true and new devotion to Mary, to be well-practiced, depends to a great extent on great docility to the Holy Spirit and on responding to his inspirations, which is very proper to children.

This book, therefore, guides children to be aware of their Marian filiation, since they can be slaves of Mary and imbibe her spirit, so as to be able to do everything through her, with her, in her, and for her. More concretely, these pages prepare children to consecrate themselves to Mary in maternal slavery of love according to the spirit of St. Louis Marie.

To this end, this consecration book is divided into two parts: The first part is a brief explanation of devotion to Mary according to St. Louis Marie, broadly outlining devotion to Mary and how it is practiced in five chapters. The second part is a preparation that extends over the course of twelve days, in which the child will learn something new each day about Mary, her miracles and history, the life of a saint, and will conclude with some resolution or task. In this way, the child is taught the true devotion to Mary and is prepared to consecrate himself to her in the maternal slavery of love.

The main purpose of the book is that the child consecrates himself to Mary, hence, this second part is the most important. The first part should be read a few days before beginning the preparation for the consecration and can even be reread (or referred to) during the preparation itself.

Now, keeping the child busy in the preparation and his soul fixed on the day of his consecration are very important tasks to be done by the parents or guardians. Twelve days can be a long time, so adults need to help the child persevere in his or her preparation. However, the time can be managed very flexibly. If it seems necessary to increase the days of preparation or shorten them, either to better assimilate the concepts or to avoid making the preparation tedious, it is possible to do so. Twelve days is rather indicative.

Likewise, we highly recommend the children be guided in the

reading, since sometimes it can be difficult to understand. Although we have tried to present the doctrine of St. Louis Marie in the simplest way possible, it may be that some phrases may be too elevated for some children, depending on their age and personality.

We want to offer this book to be used by parents, tutors, and catechists in families, schools, parishes, oratories, and popular missions, so children can prepare themselves for the consecration to Mary.

It is recommended that the consecration be on a Marian feast day and celebrated as a very special day: attending Mass and making the consecration there before an image of Our Lady, with the prayer that appears at the end of the book, or a similar one, which if possible, the child should write in his or her own handwriting. If possible, children who have already made their First Communion, should go to confession and receive the Eucharist that same day or within the days preceding their consecration.

In this chart you can see some possible starting days with their respective Marian feasts, so that the day of consecration would be the thirteenth day. Of course, any other Marian date can be chosen.

Starting Date	*Marian Feast*	*Day of Consecration*
January 21st	The Presentation of the Lord	February 2nd
January 30th	Our Lady of Lourdes	February 11th
March 13th	The Annunciation	March 25th
April 26th	Our Lady of Lujan	May 8th
May 1st	Our Lady of Fatima	May 13th
May 19th	The Visitation	May 31st
Varies	The Immaculate Heart of Mary	Saturday after the Sacred Heart
July 4th	Our Lady of Mount Carmel	July 16th
August 3rd	The Assumption of Mary	August 15th
August 10th	The Queenship of Mary	August 22nd
August 27th	The Nativity of Mary	September 8th
August 31st	The Holy Name of Mary	September 12th
September 3rd	Our Lady of Sorrows	September 15th
September 25th	Our Lady of the Rosary	October 7th
November 9th	The Presentation of Mary	November 21st
November 26th	The Immaculate Conception	December 8th

November 30th	Our Lady of Guadalupe	December 12th
December 20th	Mary, Mother of God	January 1st

The general structure of the preparation is ordered according to the mind of St. Louis Marie. He suggests making it for thirty-three days, but here we adapt it to children and make it twelve days. In any case, we follow the guidance of St. Louis Marie Grignion de Montfort in relation to the motives and different aspects of the preparation. The general structure is as follows:

Theme of the Preparation	Quantity of Days	Text of St. Louis Marie	Chapters of This Book
Empty oneself of the spirit of the world	3 Days	*Those who desire to take up this special devotion should spend at least twelve days in emptying themselves of the spirit of the world, which is opposed to the spirit of Jesus. (n.227)*	1. Making sacrifices (contrary to self-love) 2. Obeying Our Blessed Mother (contrary to our own will) 3. Desiring Heaven (contrary to a worldly spirit)
To fill onself with Jesus Christ by means of the Blessed Virgin Mary	3 Days	*During the first week they should offer up all their prayers and acts of devotion to acquire knowledge of themselves and sorrow for their sins. (n.228)*	4. St. Peter (Repentance of sinners) 5. St. Dominic Savio (To resolve to sin no more) 6. St. Tarcisius (Even to the point of giving one's life)
	4 Days	*Each day of the second week they should endeavor to acquire an understanding of the Blessed Virgin and ask the Holy Spirit for this grace. (n.229)*	7.The Annunciation (In Mary) (Material Cause) 8.The Birth of Jesus (For Mary) (Final Cause) 9.The Wedding at Cana (Through Mary) (Efficient Cause) 10. At the Foot of the Cross (With Mary) (Formal Cause)
	2 Days	*During the third week they should seek to understand Jesus Christ better. (n.230)*	11. The Heart of Jesus (Divinity and Humanity) 12. The Eucharist (Love to its extreme)

Consecration	*At the end of the three weeks, they should go to confession and receive Holy Communion. After communion they will recite the formula of consecration. If they do not have a printed copy of the act, they should write it out or have it copied and then sign it on the very day they make it. (n. 231)*	13. The Day Has Arrived

The children do not need to be aware of the different stages of preparation for they will be given naturally by the same theme and flow of the book. What is important is to instill in them responsibility and perseverance and to encourage them to fulfill the prayers and resolutions of each day. It would also help them greatly to pray the Rosary as a family during the days of preparation.

We entrust this work and all the children who will consecrate themselves to Mary in the maternal slavery of love to God. May St. Louis Marie help us to be faithful devotees of the Ever-Virgin Mary.

Father Bernardo M. Ibarra, IVE
September 8, 2020

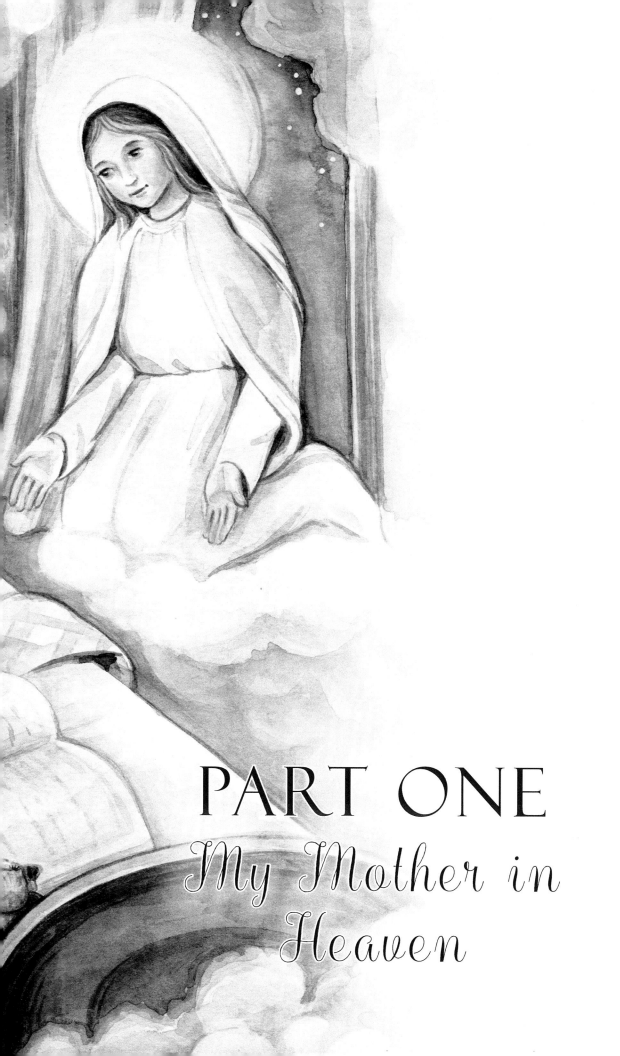

PART ONE
My Mother in Heaven

INTRODUCTION
CONSECRATE MYSELF TO MARY

Do you know that we all have a mother on earth and one in Heaven? Your mother on earth is the one who carried you for nine months in her womb and taught you to talk and walk. She loves you very much and is always concerned for your well-being.

But in Heaven, we also have another mother, who is Mary, the mother of Jesus and the mother of us all. When Jesus died on the cross for all men, He left us everything He had, even His own mother, whom we also call Our Lady. He wanted to give us the greatest gift, the best gift of all, and He found no other better than His own mother.

This is why we all have two mothers, one on earth and one in Heaven, and we have to be good children and love our two mothers very much.

How can I be a good child of my mother in Heaven, Mary? I am a good child when I do what she likes; and what she likes most is that we consecrate ourselves totally to her.

But what does it mean to consecrate oneself? To consecrate myself means to recognize Mary as my mother, to belong completely to her, and to do all things in such a way that everyone can realize that I am her child. It also means to let

Mary do with me and with my belongings what she wants to do, because I trust that she knows what is best for me, and knows better than I do, how to distribute all the good I do, to the people who need it most.

When we consecrate ourselves to Mary, she is very happy, because in this way she can bring us closer to Jesus. She wants very much for us to know and love Jesus, and since this is not easy, she herself wants to teach us how.

In order to consecrate yourself, you must be well-prepared and learn some very important lessons. In this book, you will learn how to be a good son or daughter of our Heavenly Mother and you will be able to prepare for the consecration of yourself to her. But first you must know who St. Louis Marie de Montfort is, because he was the one who taught us how to be good children of Mary.

St. Louis wanted to be a priest and a missionary from the time he was a little boy so he could help everyone reach Heaven. So great was his desire to lead all men to Jesus that he had the best idea of all: to lead them through Mary, because she is the easiest and quickest way to Jesus.

For this reason, St. Louis Marie worked hard throughout his life to make everyone love Our Lady. He wrote many books and taught many lessons about Mary. He loved her so much that he prayed the Rosary every day in front of her image.

St. Louis Marie is the master who best teaches us how to be good children of Mary and how to best prepare ourselves to consecrate ourselves to her.

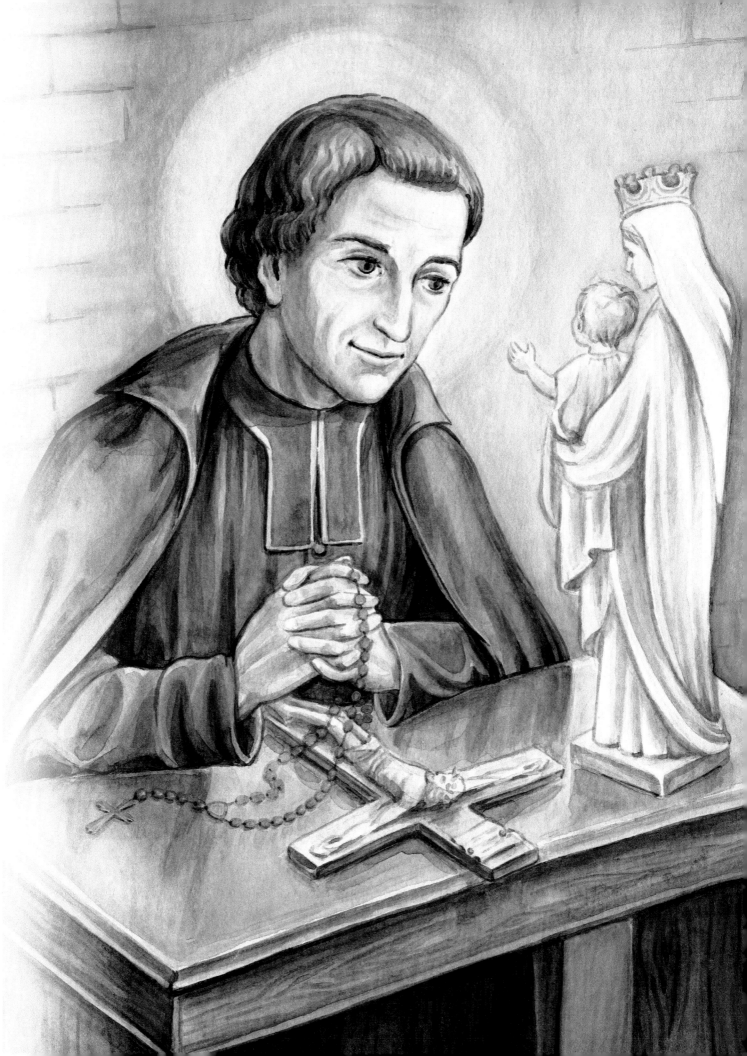

CHAPTER 1
THE SECRET WAY

As you may have learned in your catechism, God created man to know, love, and serve Him on this earth, and then to enjoy Him in Heaven forever. This is a very important truth, so important that, if we forget it, we live as if we were lost; like those who walk without knowing where they have to go.

Another important truth that Jesus taught us is that the road to Heaven is narrow and there are few who find it.

But you don't have to worry, because today you will learn a secret. It is not just any secret, but the most important of all, which St. Louis Marie taught us. But you have to pay attention so that you don't forget it, and you have to keep it in your heart so that it doesn't get lost.

The secret is that there is a shortcut, an easy and fast way to get to Heaven. There are many ways to get to Heaven. Some are very difficult and dangerous. Others are very long and never seem to end. But the way I will show you is the best of all because it takes us to Heaven as fast as if we were on the highway or in an elevator. And what is this way? This way is called Mary. She is the easiest and shortest way to get to Heaven.

Why is Mary the easiest and shortest way? Because she is the mother of Jesus, and therefore she is the one who knows best how to reach Him. Mary knows the best ways to know Him, love Him, and serve Him.

Just as Jesus came into the world through Mary, being born of her, we also have to go to Jesus with Mary's help. She is the way that leads us to Jesus. Outside of her, everything is dangerous and difficult.

This, then, is the secret: with Our Lady we go to Heaven very quickly, because she "is the surest, the shortest, and the most perfect way to go to Jesus." That is why we must be very united to Our Lady and love her very much. The more we love her, the more we will love Jesus.

CHAPTER 2
I AM ALL YOURS

You have already learned that Mary, whom we also call Our Lady, is the best way to go to Jesus. She is the secret way. Therefore, we must always love her very much and be with her. We must be her good children and her slaves of love.

What is a slave? A slave is a person who completely belongs to another person. The slave does not do what he wants, but always does what his owner tells him to do. In this same way, we also must do whatever Mary wants because she is our Queen.

But our slavery is not just any slavery. It is a slavery of love—because no one forces us to become slaves. We do it because we love her very much and we know that what she requests of us is always the best.

As slaves we belong totally to Mary and all we have is hers. Everything that is ours is hers. This means that we have to strive to make good use of all we have, because Mary would never do anything bad with what belongs to her.

And what do we have to give to Our Lady?

1. We have to give her our body: our hands, feet, eyes, mouth, ears and heart. Therefore, we have to use our whole body just as Mary would do.

2. Our soul must also be hers: our whole life, what we think, and what we want. Everything belongs to Our Lady.

3. We must also give Our Lady all our belongings. Our toys, devices, and clothes belong to Our Lady. We simply use them as something borrowed.

4. Finally, we must give Our Lady our good works. Everything good we do must belong to Mary. She is the owner of our *merits*, that is, the reward for doing good works. Every time we do a good deed, God prepares a reward for us in Heaven, which is called a *merit*. We also give them to Our Lady, so that she can use them as she wishes, because we are her slaves. Then, because she is a very good and wise mother, she can give our merits to other people who need them more or who have almost no merits.

When we become slaves of Our Lady, we give her all our body, all our life, all our belongings and all our good works. That is why we always say to her: "I am all yours, Mary."

CHAPTER 3
THE DAY OF MY BAPTISM

We already learned that Mary is the secret way to Heaven and that we are to be her slaves. Now you will learn what happens in your soul when you become a slave of Our Lady.

When we were little children—and some were not that little—we were baptized and became children of God. It was a very important day for all of us because we emptied ourselves of evil, of sin, and became children of God. Our souls were cleansed.

Did you know that when we become slaves of Mary something very similar happens to us? It is like being baptized again, because we empty ourselves of all the evil in us and we promise to do many good works and sacrifices. When we become slaves of Mary, we renounce the devil and unite ourselves to her and to Jesus.

Before baptism we were slaves of the devil and belonged to him. But now, after baptism, we are slaves of Our Lady and are always at her service.

But sometimes we forget this and do not remember that we were baptized and that we promised to be holy, obedient, and good. Therefore, we have to be faithful and persevere. Our Lady will help us greatly, as long as we are good slaves.

To be Our Lady's slave is a very beautiful thing because it makes us truly free. It frees us from sin and from our own preferences, to do only what Jesus and Mary want. If we always do what we want, we are ruling ourselves and not allowing Our Lady to guide us.

A true slave of Our Lady is a free and very good child of hers.

Let us be Our Lady's best slaves!

CHAPTER 4
MY INNER FRIEND AND TEACHER

e have already learned so much! Mary is our secret way. She leads us to Jesus. We must be her slaves, giving her all that we have and are, just as we did on the day of our baptism.

But sometimes all this is very difficult because it requires much effort or we forget. Yet there is nothing to worry about because God sends us a great friend, a Divine Person who consoles us and gives us the strength to be good slaves. He is the Holy Spirit and is the Third Person of the Holy Trinity.

As you well know, God is only one, but in Him there are three persons: the Father, the Son, and the Holy Spirit. We always say these three names when we make the sign of the cross before praying. The Holy Spirit is as much God as the Father is, and as His Son Jesus is. He is always with Jesus and Our Lady, and sometimes He appeared as a dove, fire, or wind. He is an invisible friend, although He is very true and real. For example: one day He appeared to the Apostles and to Our Lady as fire, and gave them much strength to be saints and to not be afraid to suffer and die for Jesus.

The Holy Spirit then, is our friend who gives life to our souls and makes us good children of Mary. Without Him, we could love neither Jesus nor Our Lady. He also makes us slaves of Our Lady and just like her. He is very good and loves to live in us, as long as we do not commit sin. He loves us so much that He is always with us, even when we sleep, and even more so when we pray.

The Holy Spirit is not only a very good friend, but He is also our teacher who helps us understand what is difficult to understand. This is why we always have to ask for His help in order to understand and love the things of God that we learn in Catechism. We especially have to ask the Holy Spirit to make us understand how to be good slaves and children of Mary.

In addition, the Holy Spirit speaks in our ears every day. He tells us what to do and what not to do. He is the best counselor and guide. Sometimes He tells us to behave well, to help at home, to not be envious, and to not complain. Other times He tells us to do our homework, to obey mom and dad, and to pray when we wake up, and when we go to sleep. He reminds us to pray the Rosary, to go to Mass on Sundays, and to love Jesus and Our Lady very much.

We have to be attentive so we can always do what He tells us! We have to learn to recognize His voice, because it is a voice that is only heard in our hearts and in our minds.

Are you ready to listen to your inner friend and teacher?

CHAPTER 5
TO JESUS THROUGH MARY

Once upon a time there was a peasant who was so poor that all he had to eat was an apple. And even though it was all he had, he wanted to give it to the king so that he could be friends with him. But, of course, an apple is not much of a gift. The poor man did not know what to do, because surely the king would not be happy with such a poor gift.

He thought about it and went to see the king's mother, the queen. He knelt down before her and said, "My lady and my queen, I want to ask you for a great favor, that you present this apple in my place to your son, the king. It is a very poor and ugly gift, but if you give it to the king, he will accept it anyway and will be very happy." The queen gladly accepted. She took the apple, polished it, put it on a silver and gold platter, and presented it to the king.

The king was very happy with such a beautiful gift and ate the apple as if it were the best fruit in the world. Immediately, he asked his mother, "Where did you get such a delicious apple?" Then the queen calling the good man, said to the king, "This peasant has brought it for you, so that you may be his friend."

The king got up from his throne and approached the good man, who was very nervous, his head was bowed, and said to him, "You have given me a very special and important gift. From today, you will be my good friend." And so from that day on, the peasant was the king's best friend, thanks to the queen mother who did him this great favor.

Did you know that in the story, we are the peasant and Mary is the Queen Mother? That is why every time we do a good deed, we have to give it to Mary, so that she can present it to Jesus, who is the King. In that way, He will accept everything we do. Even if our good works and sacrifices are very small and not well done, Our Lady cleans them, adorns them and presents them to Jesus and He accepts them wholeheartedly.

That is why we have to learn this important lesson: every time we want to go to Jesus, we have to do it through Mary. To Jesus through Mary. Always to Jesus through Mary.

PART TWO
Twelve Days of Preparation

We have learned much, but there is so much more we must learn in order to consecrate ourselves to Mary in the best possible way, so we will continue to learn as we prepare ourselves for twelve days. There are twelve days of preparation to consecrate ourselves to Our Lady!

This is not an easy undertaking and it takes a lot of effort, so we will prepare ourselves a little at a time, making ourselves better children, and thus, becoming ready to belong totally to Mary.

Tomorrow we will begin the preparation. From now on, you must be very eager to prepare. Today, say many times to Mary: "I am all yours, Mary."

Then say this prayer, which we will pray today and every day as you prepare to consecrate yourself to Mary:

My Queen and my Mother, I give myself entirely to you and show my devotion to you. I consecrate to you this day, my eyes, my ears, my tongue, my heart, in a word, my whole being without reserve. Wherefore, good mother, as I am your own, keep me and guard me as your property and possession. Amen.

St. Louis Marie, pray for us.

DAY 1
MAKING SACRIFICES

oday is the first day and we will learn something very important. First, I will tell you a story.

Not so long ago, in a little village called Fatima, Mary came down from Heaven and appeared to three little shepherds: Lucia, Francisco and Jacinta. Francisco and Jacinta were siblings and Lucia was their cousin.

One day, while they were tending the sheep, a very beautiful lady, dressed in a very white cloak and with her face full of light, appeared to them. It was Mary, and she came to ask them a great favor: she wanted the Heart of Jesus and her Immaculate Heart to no longer be offended. She told the children that her Heart and the Heart of Jesus were very sad because there are many people who do not obey God and go to hell. This is the reason why she wants children to behave well and make sacrifices.

But the children were very young and did not know what it meant to make sacrifices, so they asked Our Lady. She explained to them that to make a sacrifice means to do good works that are difficult and that we don't like to do, so that we can console the Heart of Jesus, who is very sad. They quickly understood.

From that day on, Francisco, Jacinta and Lucia always made sacrifices to offer to Mary. One day, Jacinta did not eat a meal that was very delicious. Another day, Francisco gave his candy and snack to some poorer children and, although he was very hungry, he was happy because he made a sacrifice for Jesus. Lucia, who was the oldest, also made sacrifices and prayed the Rosary often so sinners would not go to hell.

Do you want to make sacrifices too? Today is the first day of preparation and we are learning to make small sacrifices. For example: today can you stop eating something that you like very much and give it to someone else, maybe even to a poor person! Or if you'd like, you can make the sacrifice of not complaining about something that hurts you or that you don't enjoy. There are many ways to make sacrifices, and when you make them you must always say to yourself, "I do it for Jesus and Mary."

So today, you will make some sacrifices to better prepare yourself for your consecration and do not forget to say many times: "I am all yours, Mary."

Now recite the prayer:

 y Queen and my Mother, I give myself entirely to you and show my devotion to you. I consecrate to you this day, my eyes, my ears, my tongue, my heart, in a word, my whole being without reserve. Wherefore, good mother, as I am your own, keep me and guard me as your property and possession. Amen.

St. Louis Marie, pray for us.

DAY 2
OBEYING OUR LADY

Today is the second day and we will take the second step. Yesterday we learned that it is necessary to make sacrifices, like the little shepherds of Fatima. Today, we are going to learn and promise Our Lady to make one of the most difficult sacrifices, which is to obey. To obey is very important because it is what Our Lady likes us to do most, because we cannot be good children of hers if we do not obey her.

A long time ago, in the year 1630, there was a man who lived in a town called Santiago del Estero in Argentina. He had a little chapel in his house, but he did not have a statue of Our Lady. Then he thought of asking his friend to send him a statue and he did.

While they were on their journey carrying the little statue to the man's chapel, the oxen that were pulling the cart suddenly stopped and would not walk any further. There was no way to move them forward. The driver decided to take everything out of the cart to make it lighter. As he did so, he realized: if the statue of Our Lady was in the cart, the cart would not move; and if the statue was taken out of the cart, the oxen began to move.

With this miracle, the men understood that Our Lady was

telling them she wanted to stay there on the banks of the Luján River. From that day on, everybody called that little image of Mary by the name of Our Lady of Luján. The people built a large shrine on that site in her honor. Those good and simple people obeyed Mary. Thanks to their obedience, Our Lady was able to stay at that place and be the Mother of us all.

We also must be obedient and do what Our Lady asks of us. And what does Our Lady ask? She asks us to always do what we have to do at every moment. When we are praying, she asks us to pray. When we are playing and having fun, she asks us to play and have fun. When we must eat, she asks us to eat. And when we must study, she asks us to study. We must obey at all times and not just when we want to, because this is how we become saints. To consecrate ourselves to Our Lady we need to be courageous and obey even in the most difficult times.

Do you want to obey Our Lady in everything? Surely you do. But since we are weak and forgetful, we have to ask Our Lady for the grace to be always ready to obey. Promise today to obey her in all things, and don't forget to say many times: "I am all yours, Mary.

Now go before an image of Our Lady and say the prayer:

 y Queen and my Mother, I give myself entirely to you and show my devotion to you. I consecrate to you this day, my eyes, my ears, my tongue, my heart, in a word, my whole being without reserve. Wherefore, good mother, as I am your own, keep me and guard me as your property and possession. Amen.

St. Louis Marie, pray for us.

DAY 3
DESIRING HEAVEN

 he third day. We have already learned many important lessons. Today we will learn about something Our Lady likes us to do very much, but first I will tell you a story.

Not long ago, Our Lady appeared to a little girl named Bernadette. Her family was very poor and the children helped with housework and in gathering firewood.

One day, Bernadette was searching for firewood near a river where there was a cave. Suddenly, she saw a beautiful lady in the cave, who was all dressed in white, with a light blue sash and with golden roses on her feet. Bernadette was very surprised and did not know who the beautiful lady was, so she asked her for her name. The beautiful lady answered, "I am the Immaculate Conception", that is, the Virgin Mary, who never sinned. She did not even have the first sin, Original Sin, which is erased with baptism. Mary is the only woman who was without sin from the time she was in her mother's womb.

Bernadette was very happy to be able to see the Virgin Mary, but many people did not believe she saw her. She suffered much because people mocked her and called her crazy. But she was calm, because Our Lady had told her: "In this life you will suffer much, but in Heaven you will be very happy." From that moment, Bernadette thought a lot about Heaven and wanted to go there. She did not care about having to make sacrifices, being sick, or being made fun of. She only cared about going to Heaven and seeing our mother, the Virgin Mary, again.

Bernadette is a very important example for our preparation: we have to desire to go to Heaven. Jesus, Our Lady and all our holy friends are there. We, the children of God and Mary, do not belong to this world: our true home is in Heaven because that is what we were created for, to be with God and Our Lady, together, and forever.

To reach Heaven is the best thing that can happen to us, and to lose it is the worst. The most important thing is to get to Heaven, and the rest does not matter. How do we get to Heaven? It will only be by doing what God wants us to do: fulfilling the commandments, doing good works, and making sacrifices. We have to obey and behave well. If we do these things, God will give us Heaven, which is the best prize of all.

Today you will write a letter to Our Lady, asking her to help you get to Heaven, and you will tell her that you have the firm purpose of doing everything necessary to be with her in Heaven and forever.

And now, we pray:

My Queen and my Mother, I give myself entirely to you and show my devotion to you. I consecrate to you this day, my eyes, my ears, my tongue, my heart, in a word, my whole being without reserve. Wherefore, good mother, as I am your own, keep me and guard me as your property and possession. Amen.

St. Louis Marie, pray for us.

DAY 4
SAINT PETER

oday we will begin with the story of the cock of St. Peter. St. Peter was one of Jesus' best friends and was the leader of the apostles.

The night before he died, Jesus had a dinner with the apostles. While they were eating, Peter promised Jesus to be his best friend forever, and said, "Even if I have to die with you, I will not deny you." But Jesus was sad, because he knew that Peter would turn away from him that very night and said to him, "Amen, I say to you, this very night before the cock crows, you will deny me three times."

And that is exactly what happened. When Jesus was arrested before being taken to the cross, instead of helping him and accompanying him, Peter abandoned him. Just when Jesus needed his friends the most, Peter ran away and left him alone. Moreover, he said he did not know Jesus, and he repeated this three times! Peter betrayed Jesus. While he was still speaking, the cock crowed. Then, Peter remembered what Jesus had said to him and he began to weep.

Peter was weak and behaved badly. He was not brave. He was afraid and selfish. He did not want to accompany Jesus. But then Peter repented and wept for a long time, and he became a close friend of Jesus again. He changed his life and became the first Pope and died for Jesus, crucified upside down.

Many times, we do the same as Peter: we betray Jesus and leave Him alone. We offend Him by doing what He does not like. Poor Jesus and poor Mary! She too becomes sad and weeps when we behave badly and do not obey. Sin offends Jesus very much and it is the ugliest thing in the world. It is the worst thing that can happen to us in this life. It is horrible.

But, like Peter, we can also change and ask for forgiveness, and God will forgive our sins. We are sinners and very weak, but with God's help we can get up and promise not to sin anymore.

Today, promise Our Lady to always ask for forgiveness, even if it is hard and you don't like it. Light a candle to Our Lady and repent of all the things you remember that you have done wrong. And do not forget to repeat many times: "I am all yours, Mary."

Now you can say the daily prayer:

*y Queen and my Mother, I give myself entirely to you and show my devotion to you. I consecrate to you this day, my eyes, my ears, my tongue, my heart, in a word, my whole being without reserve. Wherefore, good mother, as I am your own, keep me and guard me as your property and possession. Amen.*

St. Louis Marie, pray for us.

DAY 5
SAINT DOMINIC SAVIO

ongratulations! We have reached the fifth day! We have already done so much and we still have so much more to do. Yesterday we learned that sin is very ugly and we promised Our Lady not to sin again. That is why today I will tell the story of a very good boy. His name was Dominic Savio.

Dominic was born into a very poor but honest family. Ever since he was a very young boy, he loved Our Lady very much and always remembered to pray with his family. Sometimes the older members of the family would forget to pray, so Dominic would remind them.

When Dominic started going to school, he met St. John Bosco, a very good priest, who taught him to love the Virgin Mary even more. At school they called her, "Our Lady Help of Christians".

Dominic was very good. He studied, did his chores, and always obeyed. He liked to go to the chapel to visit Jesus and to talk to Our Lady. When his classmates talked about bad things or said bad words, he became sad and stayed away from them. But when they played and had a good time, he was one of the first to be there. He had many friends and he was well-liked by them.

On the day of his first Holy Communion, Dominic made

a very important resolution: "To die rather than sin." His love for Jesus and Mary was so great that he would rather lose his life than offend them. Of course, it was also hard for him to be good and behave well, as it is for all of us, but he never gave up. If he fell, he got up again.

He loved Our Lady so much that he and his friends formed a club they called "Immaculate Conception". (Do you remember what that means?) In this club, everyone consecrated themselves to Mary as her good children, just as you will do in a few days.

We can learn much from St. Dominic: to hate sin and to love Our Lady as good children. If we fail her, she forgives us and gives us new strength, as long as we promise to not do it again, and have the firm resolution to die rather than sin.

Today's task is very easy. You should get paper and pencil and write: "To die rather than sin." Then, put the paper near your bed, so that when you get up and go to sleep, you will remember the story of St. Dominic. Don't forget to repeat many times, "I am all yours, Mary" and ask Our Lady to grant you the grace to never commit a mortal sin.

Now, you can pray

 y Queen and my Mother, I give myself entirely to you and show my devotion to you. I consecrate to you this day, my eyes, my ears, my tongue, my heart, in a word, my whole being without reserve. Wherefore, good mother, as I am your own, keep me and guard me as your property and possession. Amen.

St. Louis Marie, pray for us.

DAY 6
SAINT TARCISIUS

Congratulations! We have reached the halfway point. The consecration to Our Lady is very close. Take courage! We must keep moving, persevering in our preparation, never allowing ourselves be overcome by laziness or forgetfulness. Good children of Mary always remember her, pray to her every day, and love her very much. That's why you have to persevere and be very brave, as brave as Saint Tarcisius. Do you know who St. Tarcisius is? Today, I will tell you his story.

A long, long time ago, a boy named Tarcisius lived in the very famous and beautiful city of Rome. He was an altar boy and he loved serving at Mass. But there was a big problem: to attend Mass was forbidden by law. If people were found at Mass, the authorities would take them to jail. The Christians hid in the catacombs, which were underground tunnels, so they could celebrate the Mass. Tarcisius always went to Mass and was very careful—nobody realized where he was going.

One day after Mass, the priest asked who would be willing to bring Communion to the imprisoned Christians. Tarcisius immediately raised his hand and shouted, "I will take it to them." Seeing his courage, the priest did not hesitate to entrust Tarcisius with such an important task.

Tarcisius went out in the evening with the Eucharist upon

his chest. He clasped his hands firmly over the Eucharist to protect it because he knew very well that Jesus was there. Suddenly, some bad men who did not believe in Jesus, appeared and began to shout at him: "Tarcisius! Tarcisius! What are you carrying there?" Tarcisius did not stop, but the more he hurried on, the more the bad men chased him, until they caught him. They tried to open his hands to see what he was carrying. But Tarcisius was very strong and would not let his hands be moved. They struggled for some time, but he resisted until the men got tired of the struggle and killed him. Even when Tarcisius was dead, no one could open his hands. Only when the body of Tarcisius was brought to the priest, was he able to open his hands and take the Eucharist.

St. Tarcisius is a great example for all because he preferred to die rather than let the Eucharist be mistreated. He was not afraid of what others would say. He wanted to do everything for Jesus, to please Him alone.

Today, your assignment is to prepare for your next Communion with much fervor and, when you receive Jesus, to tell Him that you want to take care of Him and defend Him always as St. Tarcisius did. You should also draw a picture of St. Tarcisius carrying the Eucharist. But first, say the prayer, and tell Our Lady many times: "I am all yours."

My Queen and my Mother, I give myself entirely to you and show my devotion to you. I consecrate to you this day, my eyes, my ears, my tongue, my heart, in a word, my whole being without reserve. Wherefore, good mother, as I am your own, keep me and guard me as your property and possession. Amen.

St. Louis Marie, pray for us.

DAY 7
THE ANNUNCIATION
In Mary

Every March 25th, we celebrate a very important day, the day on which God became man. As you well know, God had promised Adam and Eve a Savior, who was the Son of God Himself, the Second Person of the Most Holy Trinity.

The Son said to the Father, "Here I am, I want to save men, and I want to suffer the punishment that they deserve. I want to give sanctifying grace back to them and open the gates of Heaven for them." And God the Father, out of love for us men, gave us His only Son. So it was that the Son of God became man, like one of us, and His name is Jesus, which means Savior.

But before this happened, God sent the angel Gabriel to the Virgin Mary. He asked her if she would be the Mother of the Son of God and Mary said, "Yes." It was not easy to be the Mother of God, because it involved a lot of suffering, but she accepted it with great courage.

And do you know where He became man? He became man in the womb of the Virgin Mary. He became the son of Mary. He lived in Mary for nine months, eating what she ate and going where she went. Jesus lived *in Mary*.

We have to do the same: to live *in Mary*, becoming like babies again in her womb. But how can we enter into Our

Lady's womb? It is very easy: all we need to do is to love her very much, think of her, remember her, and speak to her. When we love a person very much, that person lives in us, and we live in them, even if we are separated and in different places. We have to love Our Lady very much so that we can live in her, within her womb. The good children of Mary always desire to live in her. We must do the same: live *in Mary*.

Today's goal will be to think of Our Lady many times during the day, as many times as you can, remembering that you are in her. Before everything you do—such as eating, playing, doing chores, or going to school—say a few words to Mary in your heart, telling her that you would like her to be by your side, doing everything together with you. In this way, everything you do will be done *in Mary*. Turn to her especially when something is difficult for you, when you make a sacrifice, and also when you are happy. At the end of the day, prepare a bouquet of flowers for Our Lady and put in as many flowers as the times you remembered her throughout the day.

Repeat many times during the day, "I am all yours, Mary."

My Queen and my Mother, I give myself entirely to you and show my devotion to you. I consecrate to you this day, my eyes, my ears, my tongue, my heart, in a word, my whole being without reserve. Wherefore, good mother, as I am your own, keep me and guard me as your property and possession. Amen.

St. Louis Marie, pray for us.

DAY 8
THE NATIVITY
For Mary

fter nine months, Jesus was finally born in Bethlehem on December 25th. As you well know, every year we celebrate Christmas on Jesus' birthday.

Do you know the story of Jesus' birth? Surely you do, but I will tell it again, because it is very beautiful.

When the Virgin Mary was about to give birth to Jesus, St. Joseph took her to Bethlehem. But when they arrived in this tiny town, they found no place where the baby Jesus could be born, so they had to go to a cave, or stable, where the animals slept. Cows, donkeys, and sheep were the company of the newborn Jesus. The night was very cold, and there was no cradle in which to lay the baby Jesus, so Mary placed Him in a manger, which is the place from which the animals eat. Although the Virgin Mary and St. Joseph would have liked to give Jesus a better place to be born, they were happy because the Savior was born, the one who came to open the gates of Heaven. Upon Jesus' birth, angels came to sing and shepherds arrived to adore Him.

Now try to imagine that you are also there, next to the little baby Jesus, Our Lady and St. Joseph. They need your help. Our Lady is tired and very cold. Do you want to help her?

You have to become a little slave. Can you do it?

This will be very good for you, because it will teach you that a true son or daughter of Our Lady does everything for Mary. What does it mean to do everything *for Mary*? It means to offer her all our life and offer her everything we do. May everything we do, be a gift to her. From the time we get up and pray, until the time we go to sleep, there are many moments that can be transformed into gifts for Our Lady. You just need to give them to her and tell her, "I am all yours, Mary."

Today's goal will be to offer to Our Lady many good works and sacrifices, especially those that please her more, such as being obedient to your parents, generous with your belongings, and always being cheerful. You can also offer her that which is most difficult for you, such as getting up quickly in the morning, eating something you don't like, and doing your chores or homework.

To remember what you have learned today, put together a Nativity scene at home. Today is Christmas Day for you and you are Mary's slave.

Now say the daily prayer:

My Queen and my Mother, I give myself entirely to you and show my devotion to you. I consecrate to you this day, my eyes, my ears, my tongue, my heart, in a word, my whole being without reserve. Wherefore, good mother, as I am your own, keep me and guard me as your property and possession. Amen.

St. Louis Marie, pray for us.

DAY 9
THE WEDDING AT CANA
Through Mary

ou are very close to consecrating yourself entirely to Our Lady, and of course, I have another story to tell.

One day, Jesus and Mary were invited to the wedding of some friends. It was a very joyful celebration with singing and dancing. Suddenly, they realized that the wine had run out and that the guests had nothing left to drink. What awful news! The party would be over and everyone would have to go home disappointed.

Our Lady was quick to see the problem and wanted to remedy it. She called to Jesus and said, "They have no wine." With these words, Our Lady was asking Jesus to perform a miracle and solve the problem. Our Lady then called the servants and told them to do whatever Jesus told them to do. And what did Jesus say? He told them to fill very large jars with water and take them to the bride and groom. When they served the water from the jars, the servants realized that it was no longer water, but wine. A miracle! The water had turned into wine! The bride and groom, the relatives and the guests, were all very happy and amazed.

This story is very important because it teaches us, that in order to do good works, we have to obey Mary, that is, we have to do everything *through Mary*. Since Our Lady is our mother, we have to do things as if she herself is asking us to do them, because that is how it really is. If we play, let it be because she is asking us to do so. If we pray or go to school, let it be because she wants us to. Let us do everything *through Mary*, as her best children and slaves, just like the servants at the wedding at Cana.

Today's resolution will be to tell Our Lady before and after everything you do, that you do it for her. Then take a piece of paper and write down a list of everything you did during the day. You will give it to Our Lady, telling her with your words that you are doing everything for her. Say to her, "I am all yours, Mary" and pray:

My Queen and my Mother, I give myself entirely to you and show my devotion to you. I consecrate to you this day, my eyes, my ears, my tongue, my heart, in a word, my whole being without reserve. Wherefore, good mother, as I am your own, keep me and guard me as your property and possession. Amen.

St. Louis Marie, pray for us.

DAY 10
AT THE FOOT OF THE CROSS
With Mary

Among the last words Jesus said on the Cross were: "Here is your mother." With these words He gave us His Mother, so that she might also be our Mother. Jesus was suffering much. His hands and feet were nailed to the cross. Blood poured out of the many wounds that had been inflicted on Him. He suffered much for us and for our sins.

Yet Jesus was not thinking of Himself. He was thinking of us, and He gave us the best gift of all: His Mother.

Where was Our Lady when Jesus was dying? She was at the foot of the Cross, very close to Him. She did not speak nor complain. She suffered much, but in silence. She did not throw tantrums or make a long face. She knew that Jesus was dying for all of us and so she accepted such great suffering.

But this was not all. Our Lady also suffered with Jesus and wanted to do the same as Jesus, to save us together with Him. She united her sufferings and sorrows to those of Jesus, in such a way that they both suffered. They were as one heart and one soul. They loved each other so much that one suffered with the other!

We must do the same. We must imitate Our Lady in

everything, just as she did with Jesus. She is the best model. That's why, every time we do something, we must ask ourselves: "How would Our Lady do it?" How would Our Lady help at home? How would Our Lady play? How would Our Lady do her homework? How would Our Lady pray? Remember, everything you do should be done as Our Lady would do it. In this way you will be a good child and you will be able to do your consecration in the best way possible.

When we act in this way, we say that we do everything *with Mary*. What does it mean, then, to do everything *with Mary*? It means imitating her in everything.

For today's resolution, strive to look like Our Lady in everything you do. Think about how Our Lady would have been at your age and imitate her in everything. You can carry a holy card of Our Lady with you during this day to help you remember your resolution.

To remember what you have learned today, find some sticks and make a cross. Then, find an image of Our Lady and place it at the foot of the cross.

Repeat many times, "I am all yours, Mary" and pray:

y Queen and my Mother, I give myself entirely to you and show my devotion to you. I consecrate to you this day, my eyes, my ears, my tongue, my heart, in a word, my whole being without reserve. Wherefore, good mother, as I am your own, keep me and guard me as your property and possession. Amen.

St. Louis Marie, pray for us.

DAY 11
THE HEART OF JESUS

he big day is just around the corner! There are only two days left and these are very important days. Do you remember that consecration to Our Lady is the easiest way to reach Jesus? The more we know and love Our Lady, the more we will know and love Jesus. Our Lady leads us very quickly to Him. She is a shortcut.

And who is Jesus? You already know very well that Jesus is the son of God and the son of Mary. Jesus is man and God at the same time. As a man, He was hungry, thirsty, tired, slept, and also wept. As God, He walked on water, calmed storms, and made the blind see.

Jesus is God and man, and we discover this great truth when we look at His Heart. His Heart is like ours, but it is also the Heart of God! That is why his Heart is very special, because it is that of a man, like us, but it loves with the love of God. This leads us to another story, one that reveals to us the feelings of the Heart of Jesus.

Once upon a time, there was a very good and prayerful little nun. Her name was Margaret Mary. One day when she was praying in the chapel, Jesus appeared to her, holding in His hand his pierced Heart with a crown of thorns and fire, and He said to Margaret Mary, "This is the heart that loves men very much, but receives only offenses and ingratitude in return." She understood this very well. Jesus revealed Himself to her holding His wounded Heart, because He was very sad that many people forget Him, commit sins, and offend Him. And so, on that very day, Margaret decided to love Jesus very much so that she could console Him.

We all need to console Jesus, just as Margaret Mary did, and just as Our Lady did. And how do we console Him? It is very easy. Love those who do not love, pray for those who do not pray, make sacrifices for those who do not make sacrifices, and behave well for those who do not behave well. In this way, by uniting your own little "thorns", or efforts, to those of the Heart of Jesus, you will alleviate his pains.

As a resolution today, you will make some sacrifice to console Jesus. Help at home, share your things, or stop doing something you like, and offer a prayer for the poor sinners who do not love Jesus and Mary.

And now, we pray:

y Queen and my Mother, I give myself entirely to you and show my devotion to you. I consecrate to you this day, my eyes, my ears, my tongue, my heart, in a word, my whole being without reserve. Wherefore, good mother, as I am your own, keep me and guard me as your property and possession. Amen.

St. Louis Marie, pray for us.

DAY 12
THE EUCHARIST

oday is the last day of preparation. Tomorrow will be your consecration, which is a very, very special day. Today, then, I will tell the last story.

At every Holy Mass, when the priest lifts the host and the chalice, and we all kneel and the bell rings, Jesus becomes present: whole, real and true. But once, in the little town of Lanciano, Italy, it happened that there was a priest who doubted this, and so he celebrated Mass unwillingly. Then one day, when he lifted the host during Mass, he suddenly saw that it was no longer white but had turned red, and the wine had become the color of blood.

The bread and wine had become, as always, the Body and Blood of Jesus, but this time the miracle had been performed in a visible way, so the priest would believe. The priest was frightened and did not know what to do. Then, he began to thank God for this miracle through which he had regained faith in the real presence of Jesus in the Eucharist. He wept because he had doubted that at every Mass the bread is transformed into the Body of Jesus and the wine into his Blood.

Why is Jesus in the Eucharist? Jesus is there to show us how much He loves us. He loves us so much that He wants to be our food. He wants us to consume Him, because He wants to be very close to us. No one loves us as much as Jesus does. He died for us and then ascended into heaven, but because He did not want to leave us alone, He remains in the Eucharist.

And you, what will you do for Him? When you receive Jesus in Communion, think that you are receiving the same Jesus who was born in Bethlehem, worked in Nazareth, taught, healed the sick, worked miracles in fields and cities, died on the Cross to save us, rose from the dead, and ascended into Heaven. That same adorable and great Lord comes into our souls and enters into us to give us His grace, to save us and to make us holy. We must receive Him filled with joy, and at that moment, be so attentive, and think only of Him, and speak to Him as the best of friends.

Now that you have finished your preparation and tomorrow you will make your consecration, you must decide to be very good, to be a great saint, and an excellent son or daughter of Mary.

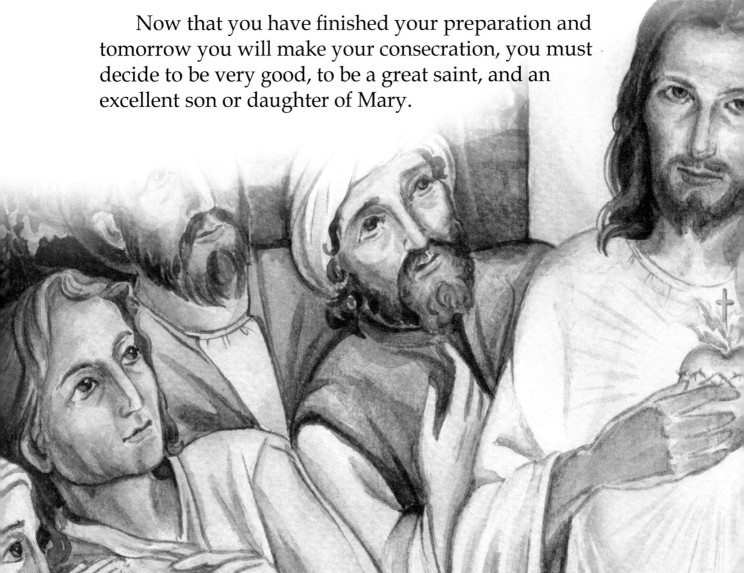

Are you ready for your consecration? The resolution for this last day will be to make a visit to Jesus in a tabernacle at a church that you have near your home. You will write a letter to Jesus, thanking Him for becoming food for you. With much trust and love, ask Him for everything you want, but above all, ask Him to make you a saint and to give you the grace to receive Him always in Holy Communion with much love.

As always, remember on this last day to say our favorite phrase, "I am all yours, Mary." And now we pray:

My Queen and my Mother, I give myself entirely to you and show my devotion to you. I consecrate to you this day, my eyes, my ears, my tongue, my heart, in a word, my whole being without reserve. Wherefore, good mother, as I am your own, keep me and guard me as your property and possession. Amen.

St. Louis Marie, pray for us.

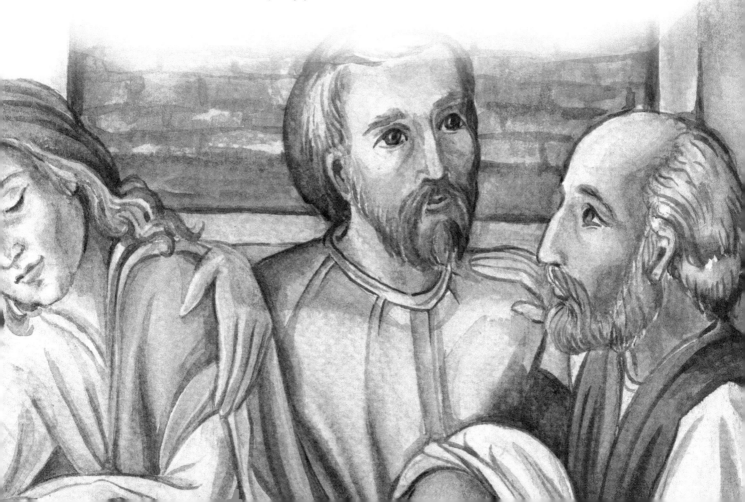

THE DAY
HAS ARRIVED
of My Consecration

YOURS FOREVER

ongratulations, the day has come! Today, you will make your consecration! From today on, you will be all for Mary and you will be ready to do everything in, for, through and with Mary!

Today, you have to trust Mary very much and put all your hope in she who is your good mother and never abandons you. From today on, you will be her slave, an excellent son or daughter of Mary. She will do her part. She will protect you, guide you, and pray for you before Jesus. You must also do your part by being a good and obedient child who makes sacrifices and has a great desire to love her with all your heart.

Always remember what St. Louis Marie taught us: "Whoever God wants to become very holy, He makes him very devoted to the Virgin Mary." Today, you will go to Mass and pay close attention. If you have already made your First Communion, ask the priest for confession and then receive Jesus in the Eucharist. When you have received Him, ask Him to take care of you and help you to be a good child of Our Lady, just as He was.

After Mass, go before an image of Our Lady and say this prayer, or one that is similar, with which you will consecrate yourself to her forever. Write it yourself and put the date of this important day. Then, sign it with your name.

O h my Lady and my Mother! When your son Jesus died on the Cross for all of us, he asked you to be my mother, to take care of me and help me to be a great saint; and right there, He commanded me to be a good, obedient and self-sacrificing child of yours.

So now, after these days of preparation, I consecrate myself to you forever, as your slave and good child, to obey you and love you in everything. I renounce sin and evil in me and I promise to do everything in you, for you, through you, and with you.

All that is mine is yours: my eyes, my ears, my tongue and my whole heart; in a word, my whole being.

I give myself completely to you and I want only to do what you want me to do. From now on, I am all yours, Mary. I am your child and slave.

Amen

When you finish praying this prayer, you can bring flowers to Our Lady or light a candle to thank her for accepting you as her child and slave. Wear a medal of Our Lady around your neck and promise to pray three Hail Marys every night.

Today is a very special day. You have to celebrate and remember it all your life. Every year you should make this same preparation and consecrate yourself to Our Lady again so that you will never forget that you are all for Mary.

50 ROSES FOR MARY

id you know that each bead of the Rosary is a rose that we give to Mary? Our Heavenly Mother loves it when we give her these roses, which are fifty Hail Marys.

A long time ago in Spain, there was a very good priest. His name was Domingo de Guzman and he loved Our Lady very much. But he was very sad, because many people where he lived were not Catholic and said false and bad things about the Blessed Virgin Mary. Domingo asked them not to say such things and preached the truth to them, but they did not listen to him, and he was more and more grieved that his Mother was offended in this way. One day, while he was thinking how he could convert these souls, Our Lady appeared to him and gave him a Rosary and told him that it was the most powerful weapon to convert sinners and bring them closer to Jesus. Then, Mary explained to him that by praying the Rosary, we obtain from God all that we ask for.

From that time on, Domingo, today known as St. Domingo, prayed the Rosary every day and taught many people to pray it, and thus converted almost all the people of that place.

After many years, Our Lady appeared again, but this time to the little shepherds of Fatima, and in addition to teaching them to make sacrifices, she also taught them to pray the

Rosary every day, especially for sinners so that they will not go to hell, and for peace in the world. The little shepherds took this to heart and prayed the Rosary always, and on some days they even prayed it two or three times.

Another saint who also loved to pray the Rosary was St. John Paul II, who was a great pope and loved Our Lady very much. Although he had many important things to do, he prayed the Rosary every day because it was his favorite prayer. We also have to pray the Rosary daily, because those who pray it are assured that they will enter Heaven. The more we pray this prayer, the more we will love the Virgin Mary and be her best slaves and children. Never forget to pray it, and, above all, pray it as a family together with your parents, siblings, and friends.

MEMORARE

Remember, Oh most gracious Virgin Mary, that never was it known that anyone who fled to thy protection, implored thy help, or sought thy intercession was left unaided.

Inspired by this confidence, I fly unto thee, Oh Virgin of Virgins, my Mother, to thee do I come, before thee I stand, sinful and sorrowful.

Oh Mother of the Word Incarnate, despise not my petitions but in thy mercy hear and answer me.

Amen.

Rege, O Maria

A.M.D.G.

words to Know the WORD